WHY SOCIALISM IS NOT BIBLICAL!

David L. Brown, Ph.D.

Why Socialism is not Biblical
Copyright © 2021 by Dr. David L. Brown
All Rights Reserved
Printed in the United States of America

ISBN 978-1-7365344-4-1

All Scripture quotes are from the King James Bible.

No part of this work may be reproduced without the expressed consent of the publisher, except for brief quotes, whether by electronic, photocopying, recording, or information storage and retrieval systems.

Address All Inquiries To:
THE OLD PATHS PUBLICATIONS, Inc.
142 Gold Flume Way
Cleveland, Georgia, U.S.A. 30528

Web: www.theoldpathspublications.com
E-mail: TOP@theoldpathspublications.com

TABLE OF CONTENTS

- TABLE OF CONTENTS 3
- INTRODUCTION 4
- OUR NATION'S CURRENT POSITION 8
    - Ichabod on the USA 8
    - The Rising Popularity of Socialism – 10
    - Definition of Terms 10
    - Socialism: 10
    - Communism 11
    - Capitalism 11
    - The Demonic Roots of Socialism 11
    - Our Nation Today 12
    - Social Justice 13
    - Totalitarianism 14
    - More on Marx & Marxism/Socialism 16
    - 3 Errors of Socialism 17
    - Communist Manifesto. 18
    - Why Socialism Is Not Biblical 19
- WHERE WILL YOU SPEND ETERNITY 26
- RESOURCES USED 30
- ABOUT THE AUTHOR 31
    - SOME OF HIS OTHER PUBLICATIONS INCLUDE: 32

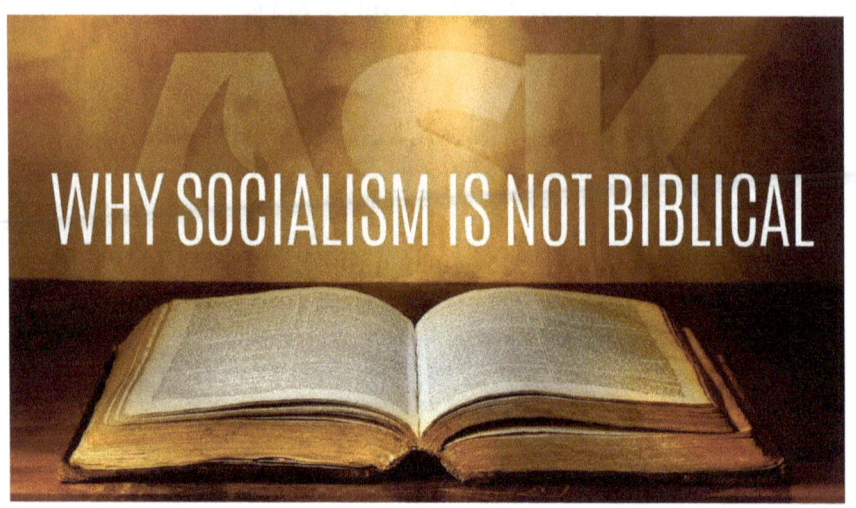

INTRODUCTION

Isaiah 59:1-15 *Behold, the LORD'S hand is not shortened, that it cannot save; neither his ear heavy, that it cannot hear: 2 But <u>your iniquities have separated between you and your God</u>, and your sins have hid his face from you, that he will not hear. 3 For <u>your hands are defiled with blood</u>, and your fingers with iniquity; your lips have spoken lies, your tongue hath muttered perverseness. 4 <u>None calleth for justice</u>, <u>nor any pleadeth for truth</u>: they trust in vanity, and speak lies; they conceive mischief, and bring forth iniquity. 5 They hatch cockatrice' eggs, and weave the spider's web: he that eateth of their eggs dieth, and that which is crushed breaketh out into a viper. 6 Their webs shall not become garments, neither shall they cover themselves with their works: their works are works of iniquity, and the act of violence is in their hands.*

WHY SOCIALISM IS NOT BIBLICAL!

7 Their <u>feet run to evil</u>, and they <u>make haste to shed innocent blood</u>: their thoughts are thoughts of iniquity; wasting and destruction are in their paths. 8 The way of peace they know not; and there is no judgment in their goings: they have made them <u>crooked paths</u>: whosoever goeth therein shall not know peace. 9 Therefore is <u>judgment far from u</u>s, neither doth justice overtake us: we wait for light, but behold obscurity; for brightness, but we walk in darkness. 10 We grope for the wall like the blind, and we grope as if we had no eyes: we stumble at noonday as in the night; we are in desolate places as dead men. 11 We roar all like bears, and mourn sore like doves: <u>we look for judgment, but there is none</u>; for salvation, but it is far off from us. 12 For <u>our transgressions are multiplied before thee</u>, and our sins testify against us: for our transgressions are with us; and as for our iniquities, we know them; 13 In transgressing and lying against the LORD, and departing away from our God, speaking oppression and revolt, conceiving and uttering from the heart words of falsehood. 14 And <u>judgment is turned away backward</u>, and <u>justice standeth afar off</u>: for <u>truth is fallen in the street</u>, and <u>equity cannot enter</u>. 15 Yea, truth faileth; and he that departeth from evil maketh himself a prey: and the LORD saw it, and it displeased him that there was no judgment."

Like never before <u>Biblical Christianity in America is disappearing</u>! While Christianity is NOT a political system, Judeo-Christian values have a foundational role in America, beginning with the Declaration of Independence:

> "We hold these truths to be self-evident, that all men are created equal, that they are endowed by their Creator with certain unalienable rights, that among these are life, liberty and the pursuit of happiness..."

Our Founding Fathers separated church from state (they did not want a national religion), but they wisely did not separate God from state; they acknowledged God as the source of our rights, and, in fact, they were careful to place Biblical morality directly into our founding documents and laws, and into our values and culture precisely to help prevent a future of totalitarian or tyrannical rule in America. The combination of keeping Judeo-Christian religious morality in the state, as opposed to the church itself; and, additionally, setting up our laws based on reason and common sense has contributed to the American Character, and to what is known as **"American Exceptionalism."**

Our Founding Fathers were religious in a new way, the Judeo-Christian way, realizing that <u>our political and human rights come from a power higher than human government</u>; they were conservative to Biblical morality. **There was and still is a connection between God and Liberty**; He is the author of it.

This belief is enshrined in the seldom sung hymn, America (My Country Tis of Thee) –

WHY SOCIALISM IS NOT BIBLICAL!

> Our fathers' God to Thee,
> Author of liberty,
> To Thee we sing.
> Long may our land be bright,
> With freedom's holy light,
> Protect us by Thy might,
> Great God our King!

The Founding Fathers were right. There is a connection between God and Liberty –

> **Psa 119:45-46** *And I will walk at liberty: for I seek thy precepts. 46 I will speak of thy testimonies also before kings, and will not be ashamed.*

Our Lord Jesus Christ reminded us,

> *And ye shall know the truth, and the truth shall make you free.* **John 8:32**

It is impossible to deny that our Founding Fathers had God and the Scriptures in mind when they signed the Declaration of Independence! He is referenced four times.

1) "the Laws of Nature and of Natures God entitle them…"
2) "endowed by their Creator…"
3) "the Supreme Judge of the world…"
4) "with a firm reliance on the protection of divine Providence…"

Then to cap things off, there is the inscription on the Liberty Bell that was rung to celebrate the first public reading of the Declaration of Independence on July 8, 1776. The Inscription is from **Leviticus 25:10**…

WHY SOCIALISM IS NOT BIBLICAL!

OUR NATION'S CURRENT POSITION

However, I fear our nation finds itself in the same place as depraved Israel in **Isaiah 59**! In 1962 the U.S. Supreme Court banned prayer in public schools. In June of 1963 the Supreme Court removed Bible reading from public education. In 1973 the U.S. Supreme Court legalized abortion and to date over 60 million babies have been murdered by abortion. In 1980 the 10 Commandments were removed from the public schools. On June 26, 2015 the Supreme Court passed a law legalizing the abomination of same sex marriage!

Ichabod on the USA

God has been and is being systematically dispossessed from His position in American culture. If He has not written **Ichabod** on the USA He likely will soon. High Priest Eli's daughter-in-law died in child birth when she heard the Ark of God was taken and her father-in-law Eli and her husband Phinehas died. Before she took her last breath she named her child **Ichabod,** which means *"the glory is departed."* (See **1 Samuel 4:14-22**).

Aristotle said, "Nature abhors a vacuum." That principle applies to our government. When the biblical principles are removed from our government change will occur. The vacuum will be filled and it is being filled with Socialism!

I am reminded what Russian Premier Nikita Khrushchev said in 1960...

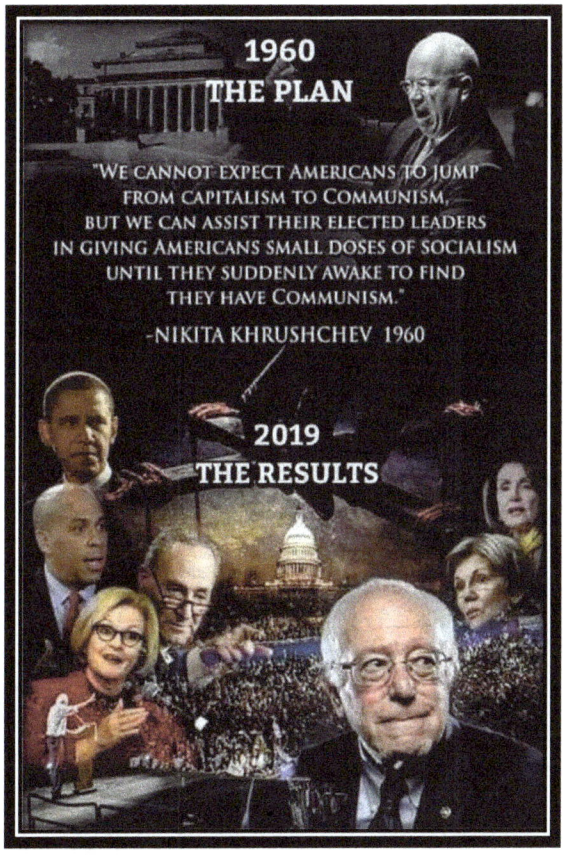

His words are coming to pass right before our eyes!

WHY SOCIALISM IS NOT BIBLICAL!

The Rising Popularity of Socialism –

A recent Gallup poll titled "Socialism as Popular as Capitalism Among Young Adults in U.S." found that about 50% of young adults favor socialism. That hasn't always been the case; that poll showed that since 2010, "young adults' overall opinion of capitalism has deteriorated to the point that **capitalism and socialism are tied in popularity among this age group**."

To understand this message we will need to define some terms.

Definition of Terms

"The term '**socialism**' was coined by French political philosopher Henri de Saint-Simon (1760-1825) as the opposite of individualism. The use of the term was popularized by the mid-to-late 1800's by European theorists, such as Karl Marx, Friedrich Engels, Leon Trotsky, and Antonio Gramsci, where power is concentrated into the heads of the state." During Russia's Bolshevik Revolution of 1917, '**socialism**' became identified as a distinct transition phrase between capitalism and communism."
(*Socialism*; Wm Federer; p.109)

Socialism:

1: Any of various economic and political theories advocating collective or governmental ownership and administration of the means of production and distribution of goods.

2: a system of society or group living in which there is no private property.

Communism

3: "The term '**communism**' comes from the Latin word 'commnis' meaning everything is held in common. There is no private ownership of anything. The government controls both production and consumption.

Capitalism

4: "The term '**capitalism**' is the private ownership of production of individuals using their own capital, with the goal for their effort being the earning of profit, which get to decide how to consume."(*Socialism;* Wm Federer; p.109-110)

Russian-American philosopher whose pen name was **Ayn Rand** (birth name Alissa Zinovievan Rosebaum) said,

> *"There is NO difference between communism and socialism, except in the means of achieving the same ultimate end: communism purposes to enslave men by force; socialism – by vote. It is merely the difference between murder and suicide."*

The Demonic Roots of Socialism

The socialism of our day finds its roots in Karl Marx (1818-1883). Marx wrote many books and poems over his lifetime. These works reveal his heart and mind toward spiritual matters, specifically toward God and the afterlife. "In his youth Marx was enthusiastic about God before being overcome by his demonic transformation. Marx's soul turned to evil." (FORTRESS AMERICA" UNDER SIEGE; by Frank Crawford; p.397). He was at war with God, and deliberately allied with the powers of darkness to accomplish his goals. (ibid. 396).

You can see this in his poem **Pale Maiden.** He writes –

> "Thus heaven I've forfeited, I know it full well.
> My, Soul, once true to God, Is chosen for Hell."

His demonic transformation is further seen in his poem, **"The Fiddler."**

> "How so! I plunge, plunge without fail
> My blood-black saber into your soul.
> That art God neither wants nor wists,
> It leaps to the brain from Hell's black mists.
> Till heart's bewitched, till senses reel:
> With Satan I have struck my deal.
> He chalks the signs, beats time for me,
> I play the death march fast and free."

Karl Marx wanted to make and rule his own world as God. German-American political philosopher Eric Voegelin wrote,

> "Marx knew that he was a god creating a world, he did not want to be the creature…he wanted to see the world from the position of God."

It is clear to me that socialism is a demonic inspired system of Government to displace God and demolish Christianity.

Our Nation Today

In our nation, socialism is rearing it hideous head by the call of liberals and progressives for:

Social Justice

5: Social justice is the view that everyone deserves [it is their right to] the equal distribution of wealth, opportunities, and privileges within a society. Individuality is done away with in the struggle for social justice. An example is the **Black Lives Matter** movement. They demand reparations for black people. They advocate defunding the police. They demand an end to "systematic racism." We have seen in 2020 that they are willing to burn, loot and riot to press their point! As one news article put it, "There is definitely a Marxist/Socialist connection with many of the protesters who currently are looting, burning down businesses, and throwing projectiles at police in several of our major cities. Many observers have noted that the huge majority of these rioters are very young people, mostly white. What started out as a protest against some policemen killing black people has morphed into some type of class warfare against "the system."

(www.columbiadailyherald.com/story/opinion/columns/2020/08/26/rowland-socialism-religion-dont-mix/3443015001/)

If you are really going to push for social justice, Social Justice begins in the womb!

WHY SOCIALISM IS NOT BIBLICAL!

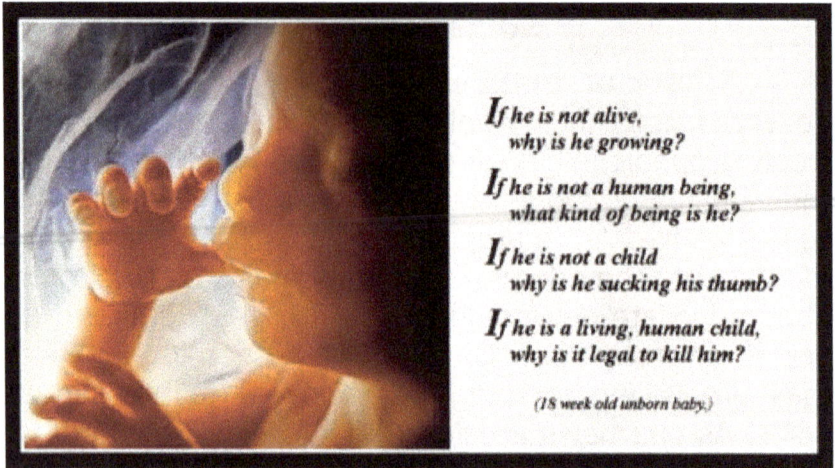

If he is not alive, why is he growing?

If he is not a human being, what kind of being is he?

If he is not a child why is he sucking his thumb?

If he is a living, human child, why is it legal to kill him?

(18 week old unborn baby.)

    Social Justice is built on the axiom popularized by Karl Marx—**"From each according to his ability, to each according to his needs."** You might wonder, what is wrong with that? But, who determines "need"? The presumably omniscient, benevolent State. Marxism promised to end the "class struggle" but did so by subjugating almost everyone to officialdom. Abolishing private property left people hostage to petty government officials who punished anyone who failed to kowtow to the latest dictates.

Totalitarianism

    6: We see that happening right now! People are being punished when they speak out against the liberal progressive narrative. The Liberal Progressives DEMAND CONFORMITY. This is *soft totalitarianism!* **Hard totalitarianism** is easy to see. They arrest you, jail you or make you disappear if you will not march in lockstep with their agenda! In soft totalitarianism, the political powers in control, large corporations, and those whose technology

WHY SOCIALISM IS NOT BIBLICAL!

(google, twitter, etc.) have become deeply imbedded in our lives punish offenders in more subtle ways. They will not publish or post your point of view. It will not appear on news broadcasts. Your ad buys will be canceled so you cannot advertise your goods or services. You are denied educational opportunities and you will find you are denied jobs, and can't even get a bank loan, etc.

Soft totalitarianism is taking place right before our eyes! If you are labeled a racist, sexist, homophobe, xenophobe, or anti-LGBT, opportunities will disappear. Google, Facebook, YouTube, Twitter, Instagram, Apple and other mega companies that now have our data will use it against us. They are using it to social engineer the culture to socialistic principles. If they are NOT stopped, they will increasingly come against Christians, Christian Colleges, Christian Ministries and the Christian Church.

A prime example of how they are doing this is what they have done to Trump supporter Mike Lindell, CEO of My Pillow. Kohl's, Wayfair, Bed Bath & Beyond and others to come are removing his company's products from their stores.

As our nation goose steps deeper into socialism, Christians will experience more persecution. Socialists hate God, they hate Christ, they hate Christianity and they hate Christians.

> **Psalms 11:3** *"If the foundations be destroyed, what can the righteous do?"*

WHY SOCIALISM IS NOT BIBLICAL!

More on Marx & Marxism/Socialism

Before we look more closely at his philosophy, you should know this about Karl Marx. Marx was born to German Jewish parents in 1818 and received his doctorate at age 23. However, you should know this. He never ran a company. He never held political office. He was never self-sufficient. He never held a job! His family lived in abject poverty. They had seven children, but only three lived into adulthood, partly owing to the poor conditions in which they lived while they were in London. Once, Karl could not leave the house because his wife Jenny had to pawn his pants to buy food. His main source of income was from his friend, Friedrich Engels.

Marx advocated doing away with private property. He surmised that capitalism emphasizes private property and, therefore, reduced ownership to the privileged few. Two separate "communities" emerged in Marx's mind: the business owners, or the bourgeoisie; and the working class, or the proletariat. According to Marx, the bourgeoisie use and exploit the proletariat with the result that one person's gain is another person's loss.

Marx believed **God was an illusion**. He felt that religion is the "**opiate of the masses**," which the rich use to manipulate the working class; the working class was promised rewards in heaven one day if they keep working diligently where God has placed them (subservient to the business owners). He was a fool (**Psa. 14:1 & 53:1**)

His answer was to have the people own everything collectively, and all work for the common good of mankind. Marx's goal was to end the ownership of private property through the state's ownership of all means of economic production. Once private property was abolished, Marx felt that a person's identity would be elevated and the wall that capitalism supposedly constructed between the owners and working class would be shattered. Everyone would value one another and work together for a shared purpose. Government would no longer be necessary, as people would become less selfish. There would be a Utopia. [Note: Thomas More titled his book 1516 book *Utopia* which was from the Greek word **ou-topos** which actually means no place or nowhere. It was said it was a pun because the Greek word **eu-topos** means good place.

There will be NO UTOPIA until King Jesus Rules in the Millennium!

3 Errors of Socialism

- **First**, Marx's assertion that one person's gain must come at another person's expense is a myth; the structure of capitalism leaves plenty of room for all to raise their standard of living through innovation and competition. It is perfectly feasible for multiple parties to compete and do well in a market of consumers who want their goods and services.

    Proverbs 10:4 "*He becometh poor that dealeth with a slack hand: but the hand of the diligent maketh rich.*"

- **Second**, Marx's theory of socialism necessitates <u>a government that is free from corruption</u> and negates the possibility of elitism within its ranks. If history has shown anything, it is that **power corrupts fallen mankind, and absolute power corrupts absolutely**. People do not naturally become less selfish. When nation or government removes God from it workings, <u>someone will take God's place in that government</u>. That someone is most often an individual or group who begins to rule over the population and seeks to maintain their privileged position at all costs. This is why socialism has led to dictatorships so often in world history.
- **Third**, Socialism is wrong in teaching that a person's identity is bound up in the work that he does. Although secular society certainly promotes this belief, the Bible says that all have equal worth because <u>all are created in the image of the eternal God</u>. True intrinsic human value lies in God's creation of us. We are fearfully and wonderfully made! (**Psa. 139:14**).

Communist Manifesto.

May 5, 2021 will be 203 birthday of Karl Marx, but **there is nothing to celebrate**. His dreams of a Utopia have led to the death of millions at the hands of socialist/communist tyrants. In 1848 Karl Marx and Friedrich Engels authored the ***Manifesto of the Communist Party*** later called the ***Communist Manifesto***. <u>Marxism in practice didn't work out so well</u>. Communist regimes produced the greatest ideological carnage in human history, <u>killing more than a hundred million people</u> in the last century.

Why Socialism Is Not Biblical

✓ Socialism is Based on a Materialistic World View Alone

According to Bernie Sanders and other socialists, <u>the greatest problem in the world is the unequal distribution of wealth</u>! His web site declared,

> "The issue of wealth and income inequality is the great moral issue of our time, it is the great economic issue of our time, and it is the great political issue of our time."

- To socialists, <u>all that really exists is the material world</u>. God is excluded. The spiritual aspect is denied! In fact, Karl Marx, the father of socialism/communism, invented the notion of **dialectical materialism** — the belief that matter contains a creative power within itself. This enabled Marx to eliminate the need for a creator, essentially erasing the existence of anything non-material.
- To socialists, suffering is caused by the unequal distribution of stuff — and salvation is achieved by the re-distribution of stuff. There's no acknowledgment of spiritual issues. There's just an assumption that if everyone is given equal stuff, all the problems in society will somehow dissolve.

WHY SOCIALISM IS NOT BIBLICAL!

Christianity affirms both the material world and the spiritual world! The problem is NOT the unequal distribution of wealth! Christianity views the greatest cause of human suffering to be spiritual in nature — the sin nature of all men. *"All have sinned..."* (**Romans 3:23**) and that needs to be rectified by salvation through Jesus Christ. Because of sin, there will always be an inequity of wealth. Jesus said, *"the poor always ye have with you...."* (**John 12:8**). Christ made it clear what the priority was to be – *"But seek ye first the kingdom of God, and his righteousness; and all these things shall be added unto you."* **Matthew 6:33**. instructed the Philippians about contentment not being found in material things, *"Not that I speak in respect of want: for I have learned, in whatsoever state I am, therewith to be content."* **Philippians 4:11**

The Bible teaches that you can have an abundant life, even if you are not wealthy. Your quality of life is not determined by how much stuff you have, but by your relationship to Christ. In **John 10:9-10** Jesus says,

> *"I am the door: by me if any man enter in, he shall be saved, and shall go in and out, and find pasture. 10 The thief cometh not, but for to steal, and to kill, and to destroy:* <u>*I am come that they might have life, and that they might have it more abundantly.*</u>

✓ **Socialism Penalizes Diligence**

Marxism/Socialism calls for the redistribution of wealth. This destroys personal accountability and the biblical work ethic. The Bible calls for diligence and condemns laziness! Consider these verses –

Proverbs 10:4 "He becometh poor that dealeth with a slack hand: but the hand of the diligent maketh rich."

Proverbs 12:24 "The hand of the diligent shall bear rule: but the slothful shall be under tribute."

Proverbs 13:4 "The soul of the sluggard desireth, and hath nothing: but the soul of the diligent shall be made fat."

Proverbs 20:4 "The sluggard will not plow by reason of the cold; therefore shall he beg in harvest, and have nothing."

Ecc 9:10 "Whatsoever thy hand findeth to do, do it with thy might…."

Colossians 3:23-24 "And whatsoever ye do, <u>do it heartily</u>, as to the Lord, and not unto men; 24 Knowing that of the Lord ye shall receive the reward of the inheritance: for ye serve the Lord Christ."

In fact, Karl Marx mooched off of others his entire life and failed to provide for his wife and children. The Bible is clear what should happen to an able-bodied person who refuses to work. We find it in Paul's second letter to the Thessalonians,

> "For even when we were with you, this we commanded you, that <u>if any would not work, neither should he eat</u>. 11 For we hear that there are some which walk among you disorderly, <u>working not at all</u>, but are busybodies. 12 Now them that are such we command and exhort by our Lord Jesus Christ, that with quietness they work, and <u>eat their own bread</u>." ***2 Thessalonians 3:10-12***.

WHY SOCIALISM IS NOT BIBLICAL!

Karl Marx was WORSE than an infidel according to **1 Timothy 5:8**

> "But if any provide not for his own, and specially for those of his own house, he hath denied the faith, and is <u>worse than an infidel</u>."

✓ **Socialism Sanctions Stealing**

This is sharing

This is theft

Dont be confused
Theft doesn't make you generous

Socialism does not believe in private property. It calls for the redistribution of wealth. Charlie Kirk, founder and executive director of *Turning Point USA* said, Socialism leads to the "seizure of private property and the dictating of individual behavior." Basically, **socialism is the theft of private property and individual liberty**. The Judeo-Christian Ethic tells you it is wrong to take things that do NOT belong to you. The 8th of the 10 Commandments is "***Thou shalt not steal***." That is in the Old and New Testaments!

WHY SOCIALISM IS NOT BIBLICAL!

An illustration of the stealing of private property is King Ahab and Queen Jezebel conspiring to kill Naboth because he refused to give up his private property, so they take it by force. Jezebel brings false charges against Naboth and he is stoned to death. Ahab takes the vineyard. The Lord condemns Ahab and Jezebel for taking the private land of Naboth (**1 Kings 21**). Ahab is killed in battle and Jezebel is thrown down from the palace tower and when they come to bury her all that is left is her skull, feet and the palms of her hands (**2 Kings 9:30-37**).

One more thought before we move on. Steve Rowland wrote in his article *Socialism and religion don't mix* – "How can we be 'good stewards' individually of our money, as the Bible commands (**1 Tim. 6:17-18**), if that role is taken over by the government? The cartoon on the previous page shows the difference between sharing and theft! Government enforced redistribution of wealth is theft!

✓ **Socialism Promotes Envy**

The foundation of socialism is envy or coveting. Socialists want what other people have. However, they do not want to work for it. **Socialists Want Free Stuff**. During the 2020 campaign we heard a lot about progressive Democrats campaigning on platforms promising "free stuff" to voters: free healthcare, free college, free childcare, and on and on. Know this, NOTHING IS FREE! Someone has to pay for it. I like what Margaret Thatcher said - Pennies don't fall from heaven – they have to be earned here on earth!

WHY SOCIALISM IS NOT BIBLICAL!

Bernie Sanders once posted on his Facebook page: "Let us wage a moral and political war against the billionaires and corporate leaders on Wall Street and elsewhere, whose policies and greed are destroying the middle class of America." (www.christianpost.com/news/5-reasons-socialism-is-not-christian-opinion.html)

Bernie is promoting envy/covetousness. He is following the teaching of Marx who saw the problems of society as a class struggle between the poor and the rich and advocated overthrowing the rich class.

Envy is sin. The last of the 10 Commandments is,

"Thou shalt not covet thy neighbor's house, thou shalt not covet thy neighbor's wife, nor his manservant, nor his maidservant, nor his ox, nor his ass, nor anything that is thy neighbor's." **Ex. 20:17**

Socialism is not compatible with Christianity! There seems to be something to that old adage that <u>when people lose their faith in God, the government often takes God's place</u>.

Stephen Rowland told this story...

> There was a sweet little 9-year-old girl who was raised by very "progressive" parents. A fellow asked her what she would do if someday she was elected President of the United States. She replied that she would give a free home to every homeless person in our nation. Her parents beamed with pride. A fellow asked her if she would be willing to clean a few homes, mow a few yards, and have a few bake sales to raise some money, then give that money to a homeless man down the street

WHY SOCIALISM IS NOT BIBLICAL!

to go towards the purchase of a home. She furrowed her brow and thought about that for a minute, then replied "Why can't that man clean homes and mow lawns himself and put the money towards a home?" The fellow replied "Welcome to the Republican Party!"

I want to issue a warning to you my friends. The current administration is calling for peace and unity. BEWARE! Is it possible that they define peace the same way Karl Marx did?

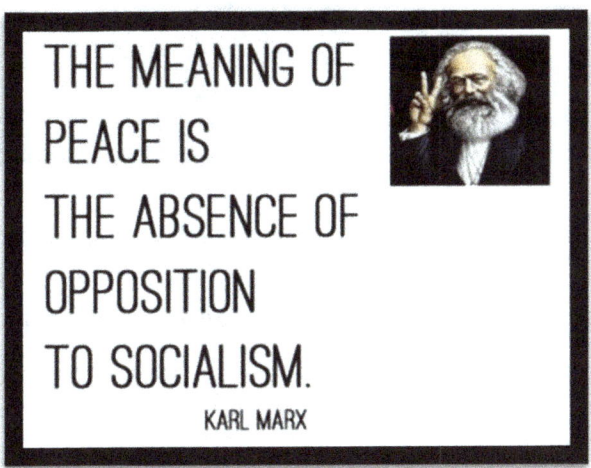

I will conclude by saying socialism is evil!

Economist Walter Williams put it this way –

> Can a moral case be made for taking the rightful property of one American and giving it to another to whom it does not belong? I think not. That's why socialism is evil. It uses evil means (coercion) to achieve what are seen as good ends (helping people). We might also note that an act that is inherently evil does not become moral simply because there's a majority consensus.

WHERE WILL YOU SPEND ETERNITY

"**Well,**" **you ask, "how would I know?"** Thank God, according to the eternity Bible, not only can you *know*, but you can *choose* where you will spend

Now we all believe – or at least most claim to believe – in the Bible as God's Word. We believe in eternity and know that life is short. The Bible itself asks, "What is your life? It is even a vapor, that appeareth for a little time, and then vanisheth away" (James 4:14).

Many claim to believe in heaven and in hell, yet, unfortunately, show little concern over their eternal destiny. We are far more concerned about this life than the next, yet we know that eternity is endless. The Word of God describes it as being "forever and ever" (Revelation 22:5).

Just think . . . an eternity to be spent forever, either in the perfect paradise called heaven or in the terrible torments of hell.

Surely we'll agree that it is just good sense to prepare for eternity now, before it is forever too late. God says, "It is appointed unto men once to die, but after this the judgment" (Hebrews 9:27).

"Well," you say, "I believe in God, go to church, and live the best I can. What else can I do?"

Now believing in God, attending church, and doing one's best are all admirable; yet, according to the Word of God, the Holy Bible, these *cannot* get us to heaven. Neither, according to God, can our church membership, baptism, confirmation, nor our good deeds attain for us eternal life.

But God has provided an answer to the matter of life and death, heaven and hell. It is an answer so simple it is frequently overlooked.

A religious leader named Nicodemus came to Jesus one night for help. Jesus told him, "You must be born again," and expanded this to include all of us by stating quite emphatically, "Except a man be born again, he cannot see the kingdom of God" (John 3:3). Pretty dogmatic perhaps, but these are the words of Christ Himself.

Some today, like Nicodemus, will ask, "How can a man be born when he is old? Can he enter the second time into his mother's womb, and be born?" (John 3:4). But Jesus answers, "That which is born of the flesh is flesh; and that which is born of Spirit is spirit" (John 3:6), stating again that one must experience a spiritual rebirth in order to enter heaven – "You must be born again" (John 3:7).

Now, have *you* been born again? Have you experienced this spiritual rebirth? This is the one thing, according to the Bible, that will determine your eternal destiny.

So, for those who really want to know how to be born again, here is the answer from God's Word.

We must ***recognize* that we are sinners,** that we've all violated God's law. The Bible says, "All have sinned, and come short of the glory of God . . . There is not a just man upon earth, that doeth good, and sinneth not . . . If we say that we have no sin, we deceive ourselves, and the truth is not in us" (Romans 3:23, 10; Ecclesiastes 7:20; I John 1:8, 10).

We must ***repent* of our sins.** The Bible says that God "commandeth all men everywhere to repent" (Acts 17:30). Jesus said, "Except you repent, you shall all likewise perish" (Luke 13:3). And it is not so difficult to repent as we pause to think of what our sins have cost God. It was for our sins that God, the Creator and King of this universe, left His home in heaven and came to earth in the Person of the Lord Jesus to suffer and bleed and die – that we might be forgiven. "Hereby perceive we the love of God, because He laid down His life for us" (I John 3:16). Then Jesus rose from the dead, proving His victory over sin and death.

We must ***receive* Christ into our hearts and lives as our Savior.** We read in the first chapter of John, speaking of the Lord Jesus, "He was in the world, and the world was made by Him, and the world knew Him not. He came unto His own, and His own received Him not. But as many as received Him, to them gave He power to become the sons of God, even to them that believe on His name" (John 1:10-12). The moment we open our hearts to the Lord Jesus and place our complete trust in Him – and Him alone – as our Savior, God promises to forgive our sins, save our soul, and reserve for us a home in heaven. Then, on the authority of the Word of God, **we can *know* where we'll spend eternity.** God says, "These things have I written unto you that believe on the name of the Son of God; that you may know that you have eternal life" (I John 5:13). And Jesus promises, "He that heareth My word, and believeth on Him that sent Me, hath everlasting life, and shall not come into condemnation; but is passed from death unto life" (John 5:24).

Now, are you willing to settle the matter of your eternal destiny? Will you do it? You can, right this moment. I sincerely hope that you will.

(Used by permission of The American Tract Society, Garland, TX)

Available From –

✝

Dr. David L Brown

P.O. Box 173
Oak Creek, Wisconsin 53154
PastorDavidLBrown@gmai.com

RESOURCES USED

SOCIALISM by William J. Federer
FORTRESS AMERICA" UNDER SIEGE by Frank Crawford
https://www.gotquestions.org/socialism-Christian.html
https://www.gotquestions.org/Christian-work-ethic.html
https://rachelnstephens.com/2018/08/02/13-reasons-jesus-was-not-a-socialist/
https://www.columbiadailyherald.com/story/opinion/columns/2020/08/26/rowland-socialism-religion-dont-mix/3443015001/2
www.crisismagazine.com/2019/the-christian-left-doesnt-get-it-socialism-is-anti-christian
https://chimesnewspaper.com/44153/opinions/christianity-and-socialism-are-totally-incompatible/_3
https://www.christianpost.com/news/5-reasons-socialism-is-not-christian-opinion.html_1
https://www.history.com/topics/industrial-revolution/socialism
https://www.peoplesworld.org/article/is-socialism-really-about-free-stuff/
https://www.blueletterbible.org/Comm/torrey_ra/fundamentals/71.cfm
https://www.washingtonpost.com/outlook/five-myths/five-myths-about-socialism/2019/03/01/692e1d84-3b73-11e9-b786-d6abcbcd212a_story.html
https://thoughtcatalog.com/sterling-terrell/2014/09/3-reasons-why-socialism-is-bad/

ABOUT THE AUTHOR

David L. Brown was born in Michigan. He came to know Christ as his Savior as the result of a Sunday school teacher throwing away the liberal curriculum, teaching through the book of Romans, and sharing the Gospel. He has been married to Linda for 49 years. She was a young lady from his home church.

David attended a Michigan University then transferred to a Christian University and Seminary where he completed a Bachelor's Degree in Social Science and Theology. He holds a Master's Degree in Theology, and Ph.D. in History, specializing in the history of the English Bible.

Since December 1979, he has been the Pastor of the First Baptist Church of Oak Creek, Wisconsin (an independent, fundamental, Baptist Church using the King James Bible and conservative music). Previous to that, he pastored an independent Baptist Church in Michigan for five years, was an assistant pastor for 4 years, and served with his wife as short-term missionaries in Haiti.

Dr. Brown is the president of the **King James Bible Research Council**:

(www.kjbresearchcouncil.com),

an organization dedicated to promoting the King James Bible and its underlying texts and other traditional text translations around the world in a solid and sensible way.

WHY SOCIALISM IS NOT BIBLICAL!

He is also the president of **Logos Communication Consortium, Inc**.

(www.logosresourcepages.org),

a research organization that produces a large variety of materials warning Christians of present dangers in our culture. He is also the vice president of the **Midwest Independent Baptist Pastor's Fellowship**, a fellowship of independent Baptist pastors, missionaries, and evangelists from fourteen upper Midwest states.

Dr. Brown is the Curator of the **Christian Heritage Bible Collection** and regularly takes his rare Bible, manuscript and artifact collection to fundamental Baptist Churches teaching and preaching on the history of our English Bible, showing how God has preserved His Word(s), and why we should use the King James Bible.

He also serves as a consultant for individuals, museums, colleges, universities, and seminaries that desire to acquire or have collections of biblical manuscripts and Bibles. He is an antiquarian book dealer with contacts around the world.

SOME OF HIS OTHER PUBLICATIONS INCLUDE:

1. *The Indestructible Book,* a 500 page, hardback with a cover
2. *The Indestructible Book,* a 500 page, perfect bound book
3. *God's Blueprint For Marriage & Family*, a perfect bound book, 108 pages
4. *The Defined Geneva Bible, New Testament, With Modern Spelling*, Editor, hardback, 344 pages
5. *The Geneva Bible, Old Testament, With Modern Spelling,* Editor, hardback, 970 pages.
6. *The Dark Side of Halloween*

WHY SOCIALISM IS NOT BIBLICAL!

7. *The 1576 Tyndale New Testament and Biography*, Hardback, 540 pages, Editor
8. Editor - *The Bible Source Book*
9. *Gaslighted, You Are Being Gaslighted,* a 32 page booklet concerning the lies and propaganda perpetrated on America.
10. *Critical Race Theory,* a 35 page booklet concerning the doctrine of devils that is captivating the minds of Americans.

He can be contacted at:
> **Dr. David L. Brown**
> **8044 S. Verdev Dr.**
> **Oak Creek, WI. 53154**
> **Phone: 414-768-9754**
> Email: PastorDavidLBrown@gmail.com

www.ingramcontent.com/pod-product-compliance
Lightning Source LLC
Chambersburg PA
CBHW061316040426
42444CB00010B/2664